HILLBILLY GUILT

WINNER OF THE
Willow Run Poetry Book Award

Hidden River Arts offers the Willow Run Poetry Book Award for an unpublished collection of poetry, in English, of 75 to 100 pages. The award provides $1000 and publication by Hidden River Publishing on its Hidden River Press imprint.

Hidden River Arts is an interdisciplinary arts organization dedicated to supporting and celebrating the unserved artists among us, particularly those outside the artistic and academic mainstream.

OTHER BOOKS BY ROY BENTLEY

My Mother's Red Ford: New & Selected Poems (Lost Horse Press, 2020)
American Loneliness (Lost Horse Press, 2019)
Body of a Deer by a Creek in Summer (Finishing Line Press, 2018)
Walking with Eve in the Loved City (University of Arkansas Press, 2018)
Starlight Taxi (Lynx House Press, 2013)
The Trouble with a Short Horse in Montana (White Pine Press, 2006)
Any One Man (Bottom Dog Books, 1992)
Boy in a Boat (University of Alabama Press, 1986)

HILLBILLY GUILT

ROY BENTLEY

HIDDEN RIVER PRESS
Philadelphia   2021

Cover design by Sara Pinsonault
Interior design and typography by P. M. Gordon Associates

Library of Congress Control Number: 2021933237
ISBN 978-0-9994915-6-0

HIDDEN RIVER PRESS
An imprint of Hidden River Publishing
Philadelphia, Pennsylvania

Acknowledgments

These poems have appeared previously in quarterlies and literary magazines:

The American Journal of Poetry: "There Seemed to Be No Safer Direction to Be Heading than Home"
The Bacon Review: "A Fisherman Casts His Net at Sunset"
Badlands Literary Journal: "Jehovah's Witnesses Descend on South Bloomfield, Ohio"
Blue Lyra Review: "Sugar Ray Robinson Leaning against His 1950 Pink Cadillac"
The Broadkill Review: "Red Bridle"
Broad River Review: "A Good Kind of Leaving"
Broad Street: "Motel America"
The Coachella Review: "Angel Wrangling"
Cold Mountain Review: "Homeless Man Reports a Dead Body by Carrying a Skull into a Florida Publix"
Crazyhorse: "Hillbilly Guilt"
Explorations '96: "In the Living Room, He Demonstrates How 120,000 Volts Protect Him"
Florida English: "Poem for Harry Graubarth, M.D."
Foundling Review: "Home Movies"
Gargoyle: "Back in Baby's Arms"
Hawai'i Pacific Review: "Under Stars"
JMWW: "Blood on the Chrysanthemums" and "The Sexiness of Older People"
Lime Hawk: "Once"
The Magnolia Review: "It Takes Exactly One Lifetime to Adjust to the Darkness"

Mastodon Dentist: "Very Few Roadways" and "After the Gauguins"
Nimrod: "The Fighting Lady"
Olentangy Review: "Mercy," "Creature from the Black Lagoon," "And They Rise, or Try to" and "Fishing the Ottawa"
One Trick Pony Review: "Badly Burned Archer Praises Fire"
Phantom Kangaroo: "There Is a Case for Interplanetary Saucers"
The Pikeville Review: "The Schwinn American"
Pine Mountain Sand & Gravel: "Reckless and Weed-wild" and "Roy's Prostate Discusses This Dark Hour"
Poydras Review: "Man Walks into Penny Arcade, Never Walks Out," "Wonder Wheel" and "More to the Point, a Lake of Fire"
Pudding: "A Place from which No One Has Ever Come Back"
Rattle: The Death of the Box Turtle"
Red Savina Review: "Taos, Lightning"
Slipstream: "Palimpsest"
The Severed Tongue: "Jerusalem Road"
The Timberline Review: "FaceTime"
Torrid Literary Journal: "Parenting"
West Trade Review: "Hitler and Goering Break Out the Gene Autry Records"
Wilderness House Literary Review: "Lazarus, Later"
Yemassee: "A Day in the Life"

I would like to thank the National Endowment for the Arts, the Ohio Arts Council, and the Florida Division of Cultural Affairs for fellowships awarded during the writing of this collection.

This book is for James Riley.

Contents

TWO

THREE

FOUR

HILLBILLY GUILT

Hillbilly Guilt

I was staying with him in his trailer that June. Weekends,
he drank. Maybe he felt his life was wrecked, though I didn't
know what wrecking your life was about. He and my mother
were talking after having been divorced for a few years. This,
after he lost a Shell station to employee theft—he had a case
of hillbilly guilt, but was working and lived in another town.
And he was trying to convince my mother to leave Dayton.
Meaning sell a house which she'd kept by factory work.
She hadn't said yes, so he was angry most of the time.
There was a picnic where he was working. And he got
smashed. I got him to leave, but he spun the tires on his
T-bird and drove like whatever godawful thing happened
next had nothing to do with being drunk and pissed off.
Which was when I prayed that he would crash the car,
that whichever God heard the prayers of scared kids
would keep us from getting there and her seeing him
like that. Meaning I was praying for them to remarry.
I had on a seat belt, though they weren't common.
And he said, later, he remembered reaching over—
at 100 mph in a downpour—and cinching it tight,
lying that he knew we were about to leave the road.
He didn't. And his waxed-gorgeous '63 Thunderbird
was the wreck we climbed out of, walking to where
I waved someone down who took us to a hospital.
I recall he broke his nose. That it bled and bled
and that he wanted me to believe what he said
happened, had happened that way. He seemed
to want not to feel what he felt at having risked
our lives for nothing. Oh, and I have to tell you:
the Chevy-to-a-hospital that stopped had a Virgin
Mary on its curving, blue dashboard and that plastic
figure said what it said about having a little faith.

ONE

Bastard

My father had a '48 Plymouth. A beast-car
with an interior a kid could get lost in. Seats
that smelled of Old Spice Aftershave Lotion,
L & M cigarettes, and gasoline. Taken together,
these were his smell. He adored cars. All kinds.
At 7, was pumping gas at a Pure Oil gas station.
Said he was in the Army (and overseas in Korea)
before he realized his gift. His mother (Susan) had,
some years before, when he was a boy, been shuttled
off to the state sanitarium in Frankfort. He was raised
by relatives who didn't agree with Susan, his mother,
loosing bullets toward a man. A married man who
loathed the world he had been handed. And drank.
Said he was not in the habit of supporting bastards.
The confluence of rudeness and my father-as-infant
wailing in blankets, throwing a Bentley fit to be held,
and my grandmother with a gun she knew how to use—
the story goes, she emptied a Colt and was reloading
when the sheriff stopped her. Maybe my dad figured
if things went bad (the wheels came off, so to speak,
as they had for her), he'd have that Goliath with the
hawk's-beak hood. He might rebuild the carburetor
in a hard rain—the hood was raised more than once,
and there were dents from his fists. To say he was
one angry man is tamping it down some. To say he
wanted to slap someone (soon) would be about right.
You don't need to love a man like that to see yourself
in every incautious step he takes. But it helps. I recall
mornings he would roar off like the road was the world
beyond maps, and pure, or as pure as it gets in this lucky
bastard's heaven of an America, and some of it was his.

Every Hungry Woman

In the passenger seat, and glad to be headed home,
to Newark, Ohio, my daughter Cait drums. Beats

four-four time. The song is by the Allman Brothers.
She sings *Every hungry woman been in your place*

before as if that pain and suffering were important.
We're on the road at Christmas because my mother

is waiting holiday dinner in an Ohio nursing home,
the room where she wobbles about bewildered. Sad.

My daughter reminds me of her grandmother: tough.
Not someone to be taken lightly. The wind picks up.

Powerline crows name the chief form of happiness:
to continue from one day to the next, and so forth.

At roadside, a black-limbed maple releases snow
as a boarded-up Shell station slouches. Grieves.

It Takes Exactly One Lifetime to Adjust to the Darkness

—Annelyse Gelman, "Conch"

My father had a raised forehead scar, jaggedly circular
and dead center. He had exited a Model T Ford through
the windshield. Didn't mind stepping into the stream
of the story: *This was before safety glass—I got cut.*
I think of the accident scar, his bright judging eyes,
as I pack to leave a wife. Kids. My sons are outside
catching fireflies in jars; my daughter begs help,
holding out a textbook on elementary astronomy.

I tell her *Not right now* because I am moving out.
Sorting and packing my half of a record collection:
Dylan, Springsteen, the Who, the Allman Brothers.
It isn't what I planned to do, but we walk outdoors
where she points to the night sky beyond fireflies,
beyond the wreck I have made of yesterday and
days before and will make of this moment, too.
It's dark. No moon. But her brothers are hunting

with a jar in one hand and its lid in the other as if
there is light everywhere around us for harvesting.
Light. Silence punctuated by the voices of children.
I hear my mother's Southern drawl, see my father
grabbing up clothes, his Westinghouse clock radio
with its hard plastic shell the color of firefly light.
I see their lives played out as small-screen 1962,
the squared-jawed American resilience of spirit

that named them as it led to divorce; after which,
they had to let whatever life comes next, come on.
At the window my wife watches as I name a few
of the stars visible in the Northern Hemisphere.
We are to have our own scar story. Inside,
I kiss the three of them goodnight. Carry
what I have to the car. All I know to do.
I want to hear music where I'm going.

Man Walks into Penny Arcade, Never Walks Out

This is before surveillance cameras, before
you could steer a CGI theropod killing machine

of the Cretaceous Period—Tyrannosaurus rex—
through cyber-landscape Brooklyn. Man walks in,

disappears from memory and reliable eyewitnesses;
is declared D-E-A-D after the usual number of years

and allowed to transmogrify into whispered footnote.
Maybe the guy fed SHOOT *the* MOTHER-IN-LAW

with Home Sweet Home gilded portraiture, aiming
at an arm-target on a circling-a-couch housedress,

a spit curled best-guesstimate of All We Despise.
Maybe he *DING-DING*ed it until he understood

how unfathomable the collapse and walked
into the remnant night. Misplaced forever.

Maybe he raised a white flag of surrender.
Maybe mystery became him in that place:

one noisy reversal crowded into another,
a red-red EXIT sign blazed and he step-

stepped as if testifying to what he saw
and the small deaths before the last.

Mercy

Take the stupid-shit kid I am, he has been
out of the air force two days and he's standing
at a cast-iron Wabash press, hydraulic hoses
snaking overhead, and it will be break time
in an hour and twenty minutes. Who is he
to leave two years before his hitch is up
and land a job in Ohio the next day?
Consider the scarecrow-thin build
of someone not fleshed out, a hairless
chest that is to bloom after marriage,
the next year. Consider the sweat
and metal shavings on his forearms.
Consider brash co-workers who wave
on their way to the metal cages of stock.
The men are loud. The kind of Loud leads
to fistfights or shootings, although fistfights
and shootings aren't new to the Buckeye State.
One of the men is wearing bib overalls and holding
a bottle of Diet Mountain Dew. If countries have souls,
some of the souls underwrite a constant hum of violence.
The real work of America is slaughter and lying about it.
Why not? Their émigré forbearers bayonetted the British.
Shot them. They took aim from cover and from a distance.
Blood spilled. Mixed with the blood of Iroquois, Cherokee.
Fields soaked it up. Rivers quickened to become red rivers.
I don't need to hear rebel yells to tell that America is fierce.
The hissing hydraulic noise of a Wabash press is a warning.
And I know not to ignore machine-gun cracks of fireworks.
But the stupid-shit Vietnam Era Veteran I am then, in 1974,
is exultant to be working Press 7 at Walker Manufacturing.
Consider the connector pipe in his hand, the cruel lighting
stamping a tubular-L of shiny steel a good-enough jewel.

A Place from which No One Has Ever Come Back

At the funeral, I fished up the strength of self
to ask *What the hell are you talking about? what*
Better Place do you think she's walked off to?

Given that we don't "fall in love" but, rather, love
rises out of unfathomable longing, comes up in us,
and we master a handful of things but never fear,
we are masters of self-delusion. Dead is dead.
You're holding onto someone and you let go.

Death's like that: just when great is in the wings
of the heart's amphitheater, under a gilded proscenium,
atria and ventricles a stage and actors performing—
about that time, we resolve we are "spirit"
and, again, we recite a litany of truisms.

As has been said: it's the middle of the night,
and we're getting up from making love, foraging
for a book of poems or a slice of rump roast—
we are bound to the body and the body
aches to be airborne. It's like the time

I owned a house in Florida by a lake. Trees.
There were bats in the roof tiles. Under them.
And I had to call someone to come and give me
a crash-course education in the habits of bats.
And since I had paid the guy a lot of money—
I can't remember figures, but it wasn't cheap—
his truth was Truth in the Absence of Better.

Same with death. Take mine, if you like,
my suppositions. It's this: we stop breathing,
absence swells and the lights go out, it's dark—
blind and sighted both stumble in such dark—
we become All That Takes Flight and Goes.
First into the palms, then past the lake:
what we see but cannot see beyond.

Under Stars

To the northwest, the continual racket and candelabra of a refinery,
its stoop-shouldered rigging an exhausted colossus. To the southeast,

a trailer park named for a tributary of the Licking River, Ramp Creek,
a fouled rivulet reduced to toxic run-off no one in his or her right mind

would drink. Each day, the eyes of those who live here open onto this.
Each night, these constellations spin imperceptibly over the real work

and those disfigured from a lack of it. I belong here, where the dead
lift off with a great effort like mallards taking flight, hugging a lake

until the splashing, skittering instant they commence to ride the air.
I do not judge you. Do not judge me standing still a while in Ohio.

Here, the terrible is obvious. Here, stars are more desperate to shine.
If a life can be said to be like a motel-vacancy sign, bright against

the endlessly rolling Universal Dark, mine has important letters
dim or altogether missing in the sign. Here's a truth: We leave

a love for one another where we can. Like any creek in Ohio
stippled with contaminants, we mirror heaven as a trailer park

and a Ford F-150 with a Dale Earnhardt sticker in the window.
One river caught fire as if it was the burning heart of the place—

smoke poured along the length of it on *The CBS Evening News*,
and I remember Cronkite saying, "And that's the way it is."

Lazarus, Later

I recall a voice. That it carried light like a lit torch.
I heard him through the graveclothes, gossiping softly
with a body, mine, and all that hovers at the periphery.
I imagined neighbors aiding my wife, her hefting jugs
heavier for the weight of grieving. I was sleepwalking

in the vision of two sons fallen sullen upon witnessing
my exit. Didn't my presence debunk doubt about Spirit
and the Almighty lacking a power to pivot between life
and reviled death? In the gospel of repair and renewal
a name was called twice before it registered as mine.

Then I ad-libbed motions I'd characterize as foreign.
Don't get me wrong. I was in a hurry to flee the tomb.
Quick to step from one imperium of flesh into another.
However, I paused a short while to let my eyes adjust.
Not to be honored or genuflect but to let it all sink in.

About then I overheard: *Lazarus, you weren't dead!*
as if there are more verifiable end-of-life departures.
Later, there were fatted-calf offerings in the Temple
and a formula to calculate the overall faithlessness.
Sidestreets reeked of reckoning and then it rained.

Necessary Violence

I drove to the hospital to toe-tag someone
who marked reenlistment by getting drunk
and overturning a like-new blue Jaguar XKE.
Ground combat in Vietnam was winding down.
I'm sure the DOA had intended to cheat disaster
but mixed the wrong chemical cocktails, titrating
a private concoction of foolhardiness and that was
that. What EMTs lifted out of a ditch near Rantoul
was alive with misadventure as light angled down,

some part of the self staying in the brackish water
to squint forever at the white beams of headlights
grasping the night air and a black-roofed Nothing.
You know his last thought was, Fuck, fuck, fuck.
I had to touch a foot to affix the wire-and-paper
USAF hospital admission tag. This blond waif
who may have shyly signed on the dotted line
for a windfall check—the man's foot was ice.
I saw him driving horizon-to-horizon 1970s

Illinois roads, straddling a white centerline
of necessary violence. Some of the fallen,
in those days, were doors closing. Some
were righteous men dousing themselves
in Shell regular gasoline on Saigon streets—
men flipping open Zippos, thumb-rolling
the wheel of a flint striker till it sparked
and the dawn-orange robes caught fire
and burned under summer-blue sky.

And They Rise, or Try To

I have two messages I've been keeping on my iPhone.
One is my urologist reporting results of a recent biopsy.
In his best upbeat patter, he reveals I don't have cancer.
At this place called Lefty's, a restaurant in New Jersey,
I play it for a waitress who smiles and starts motioning
for someone to leave what she's doing and come listen.

The other message is my father: back from a hospital,
he's been given two units of blood. Says he feels better.
A month or so before his death he says, *Love you much*
as if, this once, he wants me to know that he means it.
To be certain of anything—cancer, or what constitutes
genuine, full-on love—is to have proof or evidence.

If we're in New Jersey and you ask, Is there a God?
I'm certain of this: I was on my knees once in Ohio.
We were down to the last of our savings, my wife
and I. And so I knelt. Prayed. And we wound up
at a Catholic college run by the Sisters of Mercy.
Were given rooms in—*wait for it!*—Mercy Hall.

And if you ask why this told me we're spirits,
I confess only that I'm driving New Jersey 539
in spring in The Pine Barrens after a hard rain.
Neither side of the road seems all that blessed
as trash bins inscribed *Whiting, NJ* are hefted
by the red Mac truck stirring May ocean air.

Parenting

My father had these eyes—I mean, he could look at
and through you. One afternoon in summer, and without
waking me from my third-shift slumbers, he took Charlie,
the ancient family Beagle, to the vet. Had him put to sleep.
By then, the sad animal was falling over in the flowerbed.
Soiling himself. A mutt of a dog who lived to ride in cars.
Slept in the garage. Looked out through the glass patio door
at a world of hurt he was raja of. So when I saw my father
tamp down a mound of light-colored dirt by the phone pole,
I thought what you think at twenty-six about loss. Not much.
By then, he'd finished making the ground accept something
and he dropped the shovel. Wiped his face on a t-shirt sleeve
he'd tugged out to be of use. And I can recall my mother—
the two of us going where he was standing. She called him
by name—said Roy—like she somehow knew better than ask.
He picked up the shovel. Looked at the spot again. I knew
as he shouldered the old tool. Started walking away from us,
from the backyard, without words. On the way to the house,
I may have imagined Dad wrapping the dog body because,
leaving the garage, I saw that the quilt from Charlie's bed
was missing. Of course what he was doing was saving me—
from seeing the light leave my dog's eyes and a glaze come
over them like impenetrable fog swallowing a car's headlights.
Like the night he coughed blood, my father. Couldn't save me
a moment longer from the facts of suffering that stay with you
like the best story about someone. Someone who had lowered
the quilt-wrapped body of a dog into a hole, a makeshift but
serviceable grave he had dug without help. Reaching down,
he told us—tearing up again—as far as arms will extend
and manage their hold to drop the body into dark gently.

Aubade

Daylight and woodsmoke are without boundaries
in the neighborhoods of the poor and working poor.

I'm out on the deck. Sipping coffee. Learning
the glimpsed traceries that leaves make mid-fall.

On a deck rail, the heads of two northern cardinals
twist in tandem until one takes wing, slow-traveling

the backstories of some oaks next to an unused shed.
That one seems to need to make a song of its going.

It could be singing takes the measure of the temple
of the yard until it is the embodiment of holiness.

The fractiousness of the light through vegetations
one dominion, travels through the dark another.

Poem for Harry Graubarth, M.D.

Harry Graubarth asked me to define a nomad. I can report
my letting fly (here, I swear upon the lives of all the good
Midwestern miracle-workers like him, those who doctored
in the Gem City in those days) the phrase *One who wanders*.
Nowadays, Webster's New World College Dictionary says:
A member of a tribe of people having no permanent home,
but moving about constantly in search of food, pasture, etc.
Whatever. But I nailed it. And he knew it, having chosen it,
the noun *nomad*, because it was a word that, being a Jew,

he kept at hand like the correct spelling of his last name.
He looked as if I'd deciphered the Riddle of the Sphinx.
Tilted back in a silver swivel chair. A man with a future.
That was 1959 in a city that claims the Wright Brothers.
Tonight, years later, the cotillion—"a brisk, lively dance
characterized by many intricate figures and the constant
changing of partners"—of my life has me considering
how a gathering of words can rise like a Wright Flyer
and take flight. And have the power to make happen

what happened next, make the needle-stick to my thin,
boy's arm no big deal. I've got a hammering remembrance
of a man with the habit of letting his chair list to one side
like a ship on rough sea bound for some far-off country.
What am I to do with my gratitude for that—after year
upon year of thieving wages paid the teacher I became,
and trusting the world to love and appreciate difference?
That's the needle-stick, isn't it? Kindness before pain
then more kindness. What it costs, being in the body.

There Seemed to Be No Safer Direction
to Be Heading than Home

—Philip Norman, *John Lennon: The Life*

Lennon may have thought that before being shot to death—
that there was no safer direction to be heading than home.

If any life can be a meta-cliffhanger, his had surely been.
Now, the hour was about to be an act of black-hat ferocity,

an ouroboros wherein the snake swallows not just a world
but a rags-to-riches dream the world is having about itself.

David Geffen had called the studio to say *Double Fantasy*
had gone gold. Which was terrific. Sure. But he was happy

and had the Green Card to say he was welcome in America.
The biographer says what Yoko told him: that John Lennon

got into a car from the Record Plant to the Dakotas because
his 5-year-old, Sean, needed his kiss and a word before bed.

Who's to say John wasn't thinking that all you need is love
and a gold record and maybe a great partner like Yoko Ono

when he climbed from the limo and into the path of bullets
which then said what bullets say and *Welcome to America*.

Back in Baby's Arms

My father's funeral service was on Veteran's Day.
Korea came up. Stories of surviving winters they
called the War between the Dead and the Living.
Some years later, I recovered a phone message
saying he had been given two units of blood,
at the hospital, and was feeling pretty good.
I heard him using the tools of Guilt and Love
to get a response: "You can call me when you
get this or we'll talk tomorrow—if you want to."
And he knew I knew he had end stage lung cancer.
The asterisks of pity shaded our every conversation.
The day we drove to the graveyard a radio was on and
I heard "Back in Baby's Arms" by Patsy Cline. (She was
a singer on the Grand Ole Opry and he loved the Opry.)
Patsy was making it sound like she couldn't be Patsy
unless she could win back the attention of her squeeze.
This is music that men love to drink to: where a woman
wants back the arm-around-a-neck drape cries out Male;
where she wants his crushing hug, her lungs bursting
with a profound joy at being held that damn close.
Meaning that it's a tough country for everyone
and the earth's turn to embrace him, my father,
like that—close and closer, no space between.
I recall which song because the synchronicity
had me tearing up. On the radio Patsy Cline
was saying she wasn't complete, wasn't Patsy,
until she won back her man. When I discovered
the sound file, he'd been dead for several years.
The snows of winter-in-Ohio blown over him,
his absence the voice I hear not meaning to.

The Burden of His Gravity Lifted

—Sharon Dolin, "Sisypha Retires"

No more hearing *You could have been a doctor, son.*
A day or two from sloughing off the body, he asked me
to read to him then coughed and forgot what he asked for.
I let it go, thinking, Weren't we made to be disappointed?
And don't they say we disappointed the Creator-Father
and got booted from Eden? The Book of Genesis
says an angel with a flaming sword pointed
and that the angel spoke and Adam had to hear.
This is my burden, not yours. My father is a story
that I hear and can't stop repeating. I'm in the story.
Under a blue-and-flapping plastic tarp above a grave,
he may always be speaking. Pointing and speaking.
The penultimate message the cool, blue shadow
gliding across wet ground and these mourners.

Why James Dean Loved Bullfighting

1. James Dean with Elizabeth Taylor in *Giant*

There is a photograph of Elizabeth Taylor
looking up at James Dean making a crucified
Christ with his outstretched arms and a rifle.
There is the fact Elizabeth Taylor is kneeling,
the open car beside them lit with Texas sun,
and the front-and-center bulge in his Levis.
There is also the look of absolute triumph
on Dean's face: the validation of the fighter
at having opened a thin grape-colored cut
over the eye of the other poor dumb bastard.
In the movie, the other poor dumb bastard
is his nemesis / her husband / Rock Hudson.
This is what we mean by words like *free*.
This is how we think of you now, Jimmy,
fifty years buried, your DNA disintegrated
and the graveclothes most likely in tatters:
about to meet the eyes of a dream-woman
on her knees in sweltering heat, the rag-top
touring car running, its black door open;
in the blinding glow of lust and adoration,
about to set the rifle aside and help her up.

2. Why James Dean Loved Bullfighting

He's wearing glasses, not much of a disguise.
Standing watch on the street outside the box office
of the Egyptian Theater on Hollywood Boulevard.
He's turned his back on the crowd to start a *muleta*
with a cape of night air. No one bothers him,
thanks to his anonymity in December, 1954—
though it's *his* movie they're lining up for.
Tonight, he hears the bull's menacing charge.
Imagines himself in a suit of lights the same

silver-bullet silver as his new Porsche Spyder.
Soon, his lover (Pier Angeli) will marry Vic
Damone: "I don't give a shit. But I know how
we can cure her of Damone. We lock her
in a tiny room plastered with pictures of him
before his nose job." So what if Marlon Brando
refused to play the part of Cal in *East of Eden*.
So what if Marlon, his hero, hates bullfighting.
Tonight, Dean isn't drunk or ranting in the street
or about to slug a woman who sees through him.
He just wants to check ticket sales, his success.
Why? One bull is Indifference; the other, Time.

Sugar Ray Robinson Leaning against His 1950 Pink Cadillac

The king, the master, my idol.
—Muhammad Ali

So what if he's walking off killing Jimmy Doyle
in The Cleveland Arena after telling everyone that
he'd had this dream in which he killed Jimmy Doyle.
Never mind the routine loneliness. Years of roadwork.
This is one man the Mob couldn't buy and wouldn't kill.
Never mind that he was discharged from the U.S. Army
under mysterious circumstances after saying that he fell

down some stairs and woke, later, loopy with amnesia.
His cockleshell-pink Cadillac sits curbside in Harlem.
New Year's Day, winter weather far from apocryphal,
Ray has put the top down for the *Life* photographer.
His delight at life is in a glint of light coming off
the car, the light of New York City, a single-kiss
collective glow of promises made and broken.

Sugar Ray is looking fine in a brown suit jacket.
The one true champ kids in Harlem know by sight.
Here comes a sweep of sun to assert the start of a war
between reliance on God and trusting in the archetypal
clenched fist. Light is coming up from the car's fender,
falling on the face of one who has killed with a left hook
that knocked his opponent rigid, a sportswriter said later.

Black Cat Auditions in Hollywood, 1961

—photograph by Ralph (Rudy) Crane, *LIFE Magazine*

On the sidewalk: lots of black cats on white leashes
and Ralph Crane, who's organized the shoot for *LIFE*:

Rudy Crane and three cameras and a folding stepladder.
The animals aren't fans of movies or horror-film stars

or glacially plodding from Point A to Point B in a line.
Cue claws-out hissing off-screen, trainers petitioning

obedience with delicacies. Threats. Pharmaceuticals.
Ignore soft-tissue injuries to undefended appendages,

talk of the disposition of the bodies of offending cats.
Never mind the flood of voices and strong-arm tactics

to offer Roger Corman some portion of what he wants.
Peter Lorre is receiving a cat onto his head. Ignoring

Lorre's feline-fedora, Vincent Price unveils his best
impersonation of Joel Cairo in *The Maltese Falcon*—

an attentive Persian watches. Transfixed. Or as close
to an impersonation of transfixed as *Felis catus* gets.

Lorre is two years from an autopsy and cremation.
From obituaries saying he was László Loewenstein.

For him, this schlock work is about as rib-tickling
as the last time he kicked a craving for morphine.

TWO

Fishing the Ottawa

Once we were out of Lima, Ohio the road followed the river
past a chessboard of farmland and a Sohio refinery sprawling
in an August I still remember for its great fishing, the taillights
of a finned Imperial signing night air like an American film star

signing autographs. Like magic was being passed or was passing.
My cousins and I napped until the grab of tires on gravel woke us
and we looked out at what we were sure was left of the way there.
I remember how an Ohio cornfield touches the darkness as green

against stars, dark against leaf a wind will move ever so slightly.
We stopped. And my uncle began giving orders, good-naturedly,
as he separated out who was to transport what through the field
to the level place where we could drop our poles and bait cans.

The place he knew was near a bend in the Ottawa River known
for carp and catfish. A place boys dream of returning to as men.
"Breakfast?" my cousin Bobby said, doing his best Huck Finn.
Sure, his father shot back, waving an arm as if to set the table,

handing him a sack of day-old bakery donuts and bear claws.
Jim, my younger cousin, had begun reconnoitering the river,
the gray banks, for where he could stare away from a sunrise
he was veteran fisherman enough to recall would be blinding.

His dad put a hand to his unshaved cheek, looked us over,
a fatherly gaze finishing somewhere in the still-dark trees.
"And now?" I said. And my uncle, who had started carving
the moment down to its essentials, announced, Now we fish.

Creature from the Black Lagoon

It sat on a nightstand under a desk lamp, the Aurora model
I'd painted avocado-and-yellow so that the horror-film freak
was the last thing I saw before sleep. Kids with both parents
knelt and prayed at bedtime in Ohio in 1963. And I did too,
though a separation made sure only my mother tucked me in.
When it first happened, the break-up, my pops came around.
With gifts like the Universal Studios monster. But he stayed
away longer and longer. Remarried and had another family.
After, the sci-fi fish-as-man was our last accomplishment.
Its raised humanoid arms and claw-tipped mitts for hands
loomed, a six-pack to attest to Darwin-be-damned fitness.
I remember painting the base, red-lettering *The Creature*
as if quoting Jesus of the Gospels in the New Testament.
A still-life styrene lizard at the feet of the model snarled,
showing a prehensile black-forked-tongue designed for
snatching the beating hearts from prey. The three of us—
my 9-year-old's fears, my mother and I—said goodnight.
The battle turned to whether the light would be left on.
I didn't know what to be more terrified of, Hollywood
or seeing Threat as any movement in the dark. It wasn't
the creature's fault that what I had left of him, my father,
wasn't enough or that the unhappy water it crawled from
had neither headwaters nor shore that didn't recall pain.
It wasn't long before I ruined it. My mother at work,
the eradication of the monster began with lighter fluid—
a thorough dousing outdoors on a blacktop driveway—
and a match. I carried dripping soot-and-goo globules
to a trash can. Carried hurt the best way I knew how,
in the place a busy mother would never look. Once
it quit burning, I had taken the wreck into my arms
and hands the way the creature hefted Julie Adams,
the swimsuited starlet he, it, had to put down at last
on some back-lot clearing by a faux-Amazon jungle.

Evidently, he was tired of wanting what he couldn't have. Weary of trying to solve the central question of what, if anything, she might need except set free.

Hitler and Goering Break Out
the Gene Autry Records

Goering is a few years from being captured by the U.S. Seventh Army,
from the Nuremberg Trials and a date with a hangman whom he cheats

by swallowing cyanide. He's no Smiley Burnette, but can carry a tune.
Still, it's the Fuhrer who admires singing cowboys, chiefly Gene Autry,

in German-accented English warbling: *Where the longhorn cattle feed /
On the lowly gypsum weed / Back in the saddle again.* Goering's story:

he liberated the records from France—had the plundered crates trucked
to the Eagles Nest so Adolf, bored with Wagner, bad news, could yodel

a nightmare-soundtrack to the sufferings of millions of Polish Catholics
and doomed Jews. Now he croons: *Ridin' the range once more / Totin'*

my old 44. Goering glides into an Austrian laendler, girth shimmying,
the Pour le Merité flapping against the buttons of his shirt. The music

stops. Adolf Hitler waves for the needle to be set back on the record.
Blondi, the Fuhrer's German Shepherd, whines by a defended door.

The Light of the Heart

You'd think they were in an F. Scott Fitzgerald novel,
everything so stylized and American—the roadside
signage for Liberty Bank and an Ace Hardware Store,
the trees in no particular arrangement arranging light.
A parked car—a man behind the wheel and a woman
sighing like life is about to count again. A radio plays,
but the soundtrack is that fidgeting and looking around
amid stirrings of fabric. Maybe the fabric of Time itself
is redefined in steamed-over car windows. One of them
may know the phrase "fallen from grace" and think it or
think about why they can't (or won't) go on as they were.
However, each in turn, mid-kiss, stops thinking altogether.
These might as well be melting down two households of
heirloom silver to make a serviceable knife to sever ties.
A hand, his, is parting her legs. Her hands are busy, too.
If this is the Age of Garters and Stockings, then those are
down around her ankles. Slouched to the floor of the car.
If these know what it is they're doing, it doesn't show.
"The light of the heart"—to recast a screenplay title
from F. Scott's MGM days. That light takes over.

There Is a Case for Interplanetary Saucers

—*LIFE*, April 7, 1952

That's what it says in the upper right-hand corner
of a 20-cent copy of *LIFE* magazine. The one
with Marilyn on the cover, a white-lettered caption
reading **The Talk of Hollywood**. Sixty years later,
I fail to see the relationship between Marilyn Monroe
and interplanetary saucers. I do see that she smolders
like an exploding H-Bomb in a strapless evening gown.
If what we mean by *alien* is *not of this planet*—that's her.
And I see that a free-market promise of sex with strangers
is why America is the best country in the world in 1952.
Albert Einstein has refused the Presidency of Israel. Ban
Roll-On Deodorant is introduced. MCMLII. A leap year.
It's a year of flying saucers and sex. Cars and cigarettes.
Hemingway's *The Old Man and the Sea* has come out.
And Steinbeck's *East of Eden*. We can, and do, read.
But if the world looks to America, America is looking
at the skies or the silver screen. We're Gary Cooper
in "High Noon" in 1952. Harry Truman is in charge.
"Give 'Em Hell Harry". We're a nation of lusty men
who mentally undress wet-dream-worthy starlets—
women with unrealistic expectations of themselves.
Lucille Ball and Desi Arnaz are telling us, *Smart Young
Americans are Changing to Philip Morris—Why Don't You?*
Some of us are Cold War-McCarthyites piloting starships
named Buick and Plymouth and Ford, hitting the gas
and heading for three-bedroom homes with backyard
clotheslines and no need to question being American.
Dwight Eisenhower hasn't been elected, but he will be.
Mother Teresa is about to open the Home for Dying and
Destitute in Calcutta and war rages in Korea. Planet Earth
is one heartless place in 1952. Aliens may want to watch it.
They might want to keep going. Explore someplace else.

Blood on the Chrysanthemums

I wake to the memory of my cousin Bob holding
a tree limb, saying, *No, you first* and handing it over,
that fat branch we are about to use as battering ram.
My cousin is baptizing me in the facts of spring rain
and locked doors. We'd arrived home from school
to an empty house. It had begun to pour. Buckets.
Did I mention he liked going first—to ride a bike
or ask a girl to go steady—though he was younger?
I recall it was May. I remember taking one step

and smashing the limb through the back door
so that one of us might reach through the glass.
And I remember we got in but that I cut myself.
Not deep, a slice across the top of my fingers—
my hand must have slid along the jagged glass
like a human creature with a mind of its own.
I recall there wasn't much of a flow. But what
there was, flew from whichever hand. Droplets
fell onto my aunt's flowerbed of chrysanthemums,

the spatter bright against the white flowers, flashing
boyish insubordination as—what else—the color red.
Part of me wishes there had been applause. Because
we got in big trouble, Bob going first to the paddle
for seeing the world as the door that should open.
Bob's dead. And I feel the failure of language
and the shock of existence in the word *dead* or
I want to feel it. I want his going before me to be
that serviceable limb he handed over, smiling.

Badly Burned Archer Praises Fire

Exiting the Tournament of the Flaming Arrow,
he flashes a thumbs-up sign to the crowd.

Forget what the score is, the standings—
each remaining shooter is bowing in fealty

to what fire does, one foot in another world,
which is: to blister to the level of the dermis

as it burns in the open air. These who aren't
injured have shouldered in as if for absolution,

slightly distracted by the hum of cell phones
above the spilled weight of a stadium of quiet,

between racks of long-bows, hanging quivers,
to stand around the stretcher-bearers and EMTs

like what happens to one happens to them all.
Lines of targets gasp, concentric ring-markings

fluorescing in twilight and sign-glow. A little
hop, at the last minute, as the wheels lift off

from the ramp and collapse inward, his clothes
smoldering yet in the hands of men in blazers.

On the ride to the hospital, the archer appears
conscious and watches what's left of his life

pass by the ambulance's blue-tinted windows.
Past the greens and reds of hotel flower beds,

their managed messages nothing like smoke.
His last words: *yes* and *oh, yes* and a name.

Sleight of Hand Master Ricky Jay
& Cornell Professor Carl Sagan Discuss
the Trajectory of Cards on Mars

To the ancient Greeks and Romans, the known world comprised
Europe and an attenuated Asia and Africa, all surrounded by an
impassable World Ocean. Travelers might encounter inferior beings
called barbarians or superior beings called gods.

—Carl Sagan, *Pale Blue Dot*

If Ricky Jay believes in a pure joy of endless hours of practice,
shuffling reshuffling until the clubs diamonds spades hearts fade,
Carl Sagan likes quoting Marcus Aurelius on the relational size
of the Pale Blue Dot, preaching that all plant and animal life
is stardust. If they meet in the middle, grandly showboating,

it's misdirection wisely plotted then gloriously spontaneous.
Ricky Jay isn't much of a student, and Cornell is no circus.
There are stage lights and shadows against the stage curtains:
two Rickys and two Carls doing the math, showing their work,
forecasting the flightpaths of playing cards on Mars. Carl Sagan

posits the atmospheric variables, handing off to Ricky who begins
throwing the auxiliary deck into a watermelon half, piercing a green
pachydermous outer hide with the one-eyed jacks, the Jack of Spades
and the Jack of Hearts abutting on the round fruit skin. After applause,
Cornell professor Sagan describes the trajectory of the human future as

stagecraft so white-knuckle thrilling it might as well be prestidigitation.
Ricky Jay's shoulder-length black hair flies out as he applauds Sagan
who will never see him as the dice man Eddie Sawyer in *Deadwood*,
sporting a three-piece suit and vest and spit-shined dress shoes,
the mustached mechanic of the skill set to say: I've got this.

More to the Point, a Lake of Fire

Everyone wants to go to heaven—even murderers,
my granny says, preaching again of the Apocalypse
and the four unforgiving horsemen. No sense asking
about the vials of plague and suffering, which armies
battle against which, what infidel nation is banished
to dark Perdition or, more to the point, a lake of fire
after their defeat on the plains of Megiddo. Granny
says, *There'll be blood to the bridles of the horses.*

Of course by "murderers" she means Kentuckians
who killed her two sons in coal town honky-tonks:
shot to death unarmed since each was as menacing
as the Old Testament God. She is visioning flames,
a greedy dispersion spreading like an oil slick fire.
You see that here's one who could shovel on fuel.
Installed on my blue chenille bedspread, her face
is bare to star shine through a bedroom window,

slant snow aswirl outside the length of our street.
This is what love would offer sometimes in 1962
instead of peace—a Bible story more unnerving
than *The Twilight Zone.* For my granny, no saint,
it will never be over. There's letting go and love
turned to whatever we're left with as she shifts
her gaze from a photograph of John Kennedy
and I hear: *First, the moon will drip blood.*

Slavers Throwing Overboard the Dead and Dying, Typhoon Coming On

—J. M. W. Turner

In the painting, there are outflung legs displaying manacles.
The night is a tempest, a burgundy-black storm of corpses.

Story is, off the coast of Jamaica a captain (for the insurance)
jettisoned 132 men, women, and children. A British captain.

By 1840, the year of the Turner painting, only the Americans
and Spaniards are in the business of running slaves. However,

the artist risks everything lest we forget Captain Collingwood
and what we promise after we ask and answer right questions

about ourselves. See those reaching with small hands toward
blind-God as the truly lucky climb onto lifeboats of the dead?

Of course the fins are featured to remind us there are sharks,
a sea of teeth pearled with ovations of blood and moonlight.

Shorebirds sentry the sharks; some of the birds are airborne.
The fury of their wings makes a second cauldron of the air.

Butch and Sundance Visit Brooklyn, 1901

The Sundance Kid, known by another name then,
recalls living in unimportant rooms in a similar city.
February streets. As a boy, playing on the fire escape.
This, before he became a runaway in a covered wagon.
Butch hands a creased bill to an usher for a tiny theatre
where the camber of a marquee reads *Romeo & Juliet*.
They're dressed in formal attire. Black tie. Bowler hat.

Glisteny urban nightlife is a boutonniere. Sundance
moves at the center of the action like a species of fish
easy in the water and habituated to hiding in plain sight.
Traces the pocket-outline of a derringer for reassurance.
Etta Place is accompanying them. All of this, and more,
while Pinkertons discover the last known whereabouts
of infamous train robbers. The Hole in the Wall Gang.

They are three days from boarding the boat to Argentina,
buying the ranch and three hundred head of cattle. Sheep.
Going straight for years. And busting ass to make it work.
Tonight they're outlaws in New York, dancing with Etta.
Downing unending bottles of champagne. Sharing a box
at the theatre where Sundance instructs Butch as to who
in the Wyoming-badlands-hell William Shakespeare is.

Roaring drunk, he's trying not to imagine how this ends
or whether these doomed lovers will pull it off, the play,
with the requisite regard for what he recalls as mournful.
Gaslights blaze. Dim. Blaze again. The curtain goes up.
Etta is trying to be heard over voices from the next box.
She's saying something about Romeo being handsome,
reminding her of a small boy she helped learn to read.

A Day in the Life

Consider it: to break out a twelve-string pawn shop guitar
and launch into an original song in 1972 must have required
not just confidence. The smooth spun steel of those strings
in rough hands fashioning makeshift chords for the reason
you want—need—to hear exhortations of your own making.
The shellacked shine of the guitar body, the bruised wood
vibrating, then the vocals and arpeggios—what audacity

to risk everything in some new friend's basement room.
So what if The Beatles sing "A Day in the Life". Lennon
and McCartney started somewhere. Nets of fantasy haul in
their catch of fish from the dim few cubic feet of Ohio air.
Shoulder-length hair mimes the wingbeats of shore birds
crossing a whitecapped lake of Now. Hard not to applaud
one who scours a Burger King to the point of spotlessness

for shit wages then croons so hopefully of made-up places.
There's a break for a Marlboro, the hammers of addiction
tapping out blood rhythms as smoke seethes and flutters.
Someone shouts *Keep it down!* The work seems endless.
Like draining exhausted grease from fryers, disentangling
logistical trials in the small-town wee hours of third shift.
Like shooting black-pajamaed VC after VC in the head

or in the region of a beating heart must have to others.
Gone are the days of knights in armor. King Arthur
would sit at a table of round and Robin Hood fought
for the poor . . . You're starting in again. Same tune
but with summer storms accompanying, a hard rain
recalling what Bob Dylan said about there being no
success like failure. That failure is no success at all.

The Afterlife of Crash Test Dummies

For years they were exhaled into walls
behind the wheel of Dodge, Plymouth, Chrysler.
Tasked with defending us from extremes.

If they'd somehow been capable of speech,
there was little to announce—
the industrial grays of girders, apostrophes

of overhead light, the strapped-in world shrunk
to puppet-size, laboratory-size. One technician
did swear he thought he heard something

to the effect of *Lets do it* from a manikin
sporting a stare like that of a doorman.
If one of the Doomed had noted the hill

of the boneyard, sacrifice echoing
that of UAW laborers, a flesh of decades
crumpled like the cellophane peeled

from a cigarette pack, it would have been
freakish: something out of Mary Shelley.
If it dreamed, Pinocchio-like, where in sparking

wreckage was there a promise of anything?
Their recycled bodies make excellent outer casings
for other products. Maybe a fortunate child lifts one

up, appraising a birthday-gift Xbox in a spacious
house in a country where blissful sufficiency
floats on the surface precincts of the light.

Maybe the child wades into a surf of ribbons
and paper as if this latest extravagance
is all she has ever wanted.

A Good Kind of Leaving

A bunch of us young guys (four, counting me)
hit upon the odd notion of driving to New Mexico

from Ohio. We were in high school, and would be
in *immense* trouble. Nevertheless, we packed a car:

my mother's '64 Ford Galaxie with bald tires and
an AM radio on the Galaxie's curving dashboard.

"A Hard Rain's a-Gonna Fall" warned of Slaughter,
fallout from ICBMs the hard rain under discussion—

woozy with adrenalin, I drove all night that first
night-into-morning. Saw shapes in the headlights:

tiny drive-ins in the glow of the beams: screens
showing sci-fi films—lots of flying saucers and

death-dealing by untransfigured alien militaries.
There would be consequences for our truancies,

if we went back at all. We wouldn't be driving.
There'd be penalty buzz-cuts for the long-hairs.

Questions as to mental health, the consensus
that there was something not-right about us—

I remember Texas going on and on, opening
a forever-highway of dark-then-light while

the AM radio played Dylan and birds with
foreign-sounding songs started and America,

betrayer of souls young and old, and of birds,
sold its sweet apostasies from the billboards.

for Tom

THREE

Superman & Harry Houdini

His dreams had always been Houdiniesque: they were the dreams of a
pupa struggling in its blind cocoon, mad for a taste of light and air.
—Michael Chabon, *The Amazing Adventures of Kavalier & Clay*

According to Michael Chabon in one of his novels,
the difference between Clark Kent in a phone booth
and, say, Houdini in a packing crate: Clark Kent
is Superman and Houdini is mortal. See, there's
the fact that Houdini (Eric Weiss) has to struggle.
It's because Superman/Clark Kent is part deity—
he lives forever, doesn't lose his hair or the will
to live—that we have to concede he knows nothing
about being free. Escape is escape, certain or not,
but Houdini wins us because he's *in* that crate

where it's all about what he can make happen.
We're in there too, chafing at the lightlessness
and the easy metaphor for death and the grave.
Maybe it isn't deliverance we want but the job
of deliverer, and not for minimum wage without
benefits; maybe it's a starship the fuck out of here.
Maybe the chains are small towns in the Midwest
and maybe the crate is the soul believing in God.
Maybe the adventure begins with him surfacing,
Houdini, the Man of Steel on the banks of a river

applauding like mad what he could do with ease
by flexing any part of his improbable body or
with a blast of x-ray vision, the gargantuan chains
one more insoluble problem solved. He applauds—
Clark Kent, wearing those black-rimmed eyeglasses
and a three-piece suit—like a convert applauding
all transformations, regardless of how they happen.
He's cheering for not being complicit in fabulations
about mortality and the Spirit where the last whiff
of good, breathable air is said to smell of sulfur.

Photograph of Harry Houdini, 1899

Harry Houdini, full-length portrait, standing,
facing front, in chains. 1899.
—caption of the Library of Congress photograph

Never mind he's choreographed the camera, his pose,
that he's scandalously naked except for a flap of cloth.
Never mind the chains and padlocks, an into-the-lens
unremitting stare reminiscent of a Mesmerist or God.
Anyone who'll lie that he's from Appleton, Wisconsin
wants only to be thought an American, and one of us.

By the time they'd seen what they were looking at
he was already being raised, hoisted over their heads
by a stationary crane. They'd seen the Bound Man,
metaphor for the struggle to live, then been asked
to agree to something. No one thought to inspect
for the length of wire palmed or planted in his hair.

Not that they should have, the top-hatted shadows
or the assemblage of starvelings who would soon
walk streets of a city from which there is no escape.
No man with an ounce of decency or moral turpitude
had dared ask to insert a gloved finger into Houdini's
rectum; lift the scrotum because anything's possible,
given a leggy and buxom assistant (for misdirection)
and a bit of spirit glue. But that's beside the point.
Half the battle is getting a crowd to look up as one,
and to keep looking. From photographs, we know
that his immigrant eyes burned a gaslight-yellow.
We feel the heat after all this time. Some trick.

In the Living Room, He Demonstrates
How 120,000 Volts Protect Him

He rocks the side switch to white,
and a thread of chartreuse spark
snakes innocently between terminals
at the business end of a stun gun
he's traded for and pockets like Chapstick.

It's what he needs, lungs shot
and *tae kwon do* not enough in close
with some no-neck harvest of self
spouting off about the 47%. It's his
Contract with America that his answer

be a big brilliant stick of a wake-up call.
For long enough to make them glad the burn
goes no deeper, lets you live. He says
that the ozone smell comforts him.
I don't smell it, but I play along.

In the words of the ad: *This*
brings them to their knees.
According to the previous owner
who only used it on his own leg, and only once,
the idea is to serve pain like a meal

so the attacker "gets his fill." He believes
it's self-defense, a duty to his own life
to give back as good as he gets. The gun
is quiet again. He tells me, Oughta get one.
Then pats that pocket like a new love.

Very Few Roadways

The tire was huge. And black. And about as round
as the suddenly-open mouth of someone screaming.
In my case I may have thought, *Very few roadways*
offer protection against the rogue tire loosed and
bounding down from nowhere to cross the median.
It's the same when a terrible dream you wake from
is the quiet and stillness after a near-fatal accident
in which you walk away distrusting deliverance.
In my case, I believed that I'd been killed. Died

on an interstate outside a town in West Virginia.
At impact, I'd seen lots of frozen instants inching
toward joy—the births of screaming grandchildren,
completion of certain arduous tasks involving years
of personal sacrifice and skilled attention. There is
death and grave injury. And of course the Mystery.
A blackness looming like some great truck tire—
the Puncture-Sealing Tire For Rugged Off-Road
Conditions Like Coal Fields: the G177 DuraSeal—

in the split-second it bounce-bounces toward you.
This was like that. And like nothing else. I saw
the face of my passenger-daughter, her mouth
frozen into a wide *O* of fear. Which of course is
the ah-hah shock of recognition at what's coming
like a visitation you can never quite prepare for.
Like the child who asks the conductor where
the train is stopping next and is told "up ahead"
and repeats that as if he's naming a new town.

Jehovah's Witnesses Descend
on South Bloomfield, Ohio

The assumption is we're too stupid to know we need saving.
Too troubled or spiritually numb—too clueless—to seek God.
This one has been ringing doorbells in the bruise-black night.
Offers me a brochure titled *Can the Dead Really Live Again*.
It's Christmas, I'd take it, but I've got a dog I'm holding.
Though the animal isn't vicious, it's old. Unpredictable.
Under a whisk of porch light, the stranger inaugurates

a scripted patter. A smile is born, dies, then is born again.
I'm tempted to quote Schopenhauer, that faith is a process
involving doubt in a synergistic relationship with belief,
that the universe is irrational territory in which humans
must make a clean breast of all suspect knowledge—
"Every man takes the limits of his own field of vision
for the limits of the world." I'm open to hearing him out,

but then my dog lunges as if the Redeemed were fair game.
As if there are limits, even in Ohio, to the respect for others.
Cue me trying to be polite. Cue the retriever with a territorial
growl as deep as the wound in the side of the tormented Savior.
Cue the television left on in a room nearby, *Bad Santa* on HBO
and blotto Billy Bob Thornton saying *What the fuck do I need
with sandwiches, kid?* Loud enough for the dead to eavesdrop.

This visitor seems to want to rescue at least one more infidel.
I hold off the dog. Say *Quiet dammit* and then *Shut the hell up.*
I stretch for the four-color pamphlet. On the cover is Perdition,
char and brimstone lit as by luminaria, the smoke enwreathing
stick-figure suffering. My pissed-off dog would much rather
I let go his collar. I don't. An apotheosis of a last snarl rises.
The stranger says *Merry Christmas*. And I close the door.

After the Second Hardest Thing
I Have Had to Do

which was to bury my father—preceded by the first hardest,
burying a mother—then you died. I suppose it's good to think
that the real genius of death is that it allows absence to set in.
It was clear that you had no choice but to lie down under
egg-eyed angels. Nothing to mark your last day but a text
to my iPhone. The message: *Good Morning!* You said
you loved me. And hoped that I was all right. I said—
you were to come off a ventilator to die, your choice—
I was hoping your Wednesday would be filled with joy.

When we were boys and growing up together in Ohio,
you asked what happens when we die. Waited for an answer.
I knew so little that I used to blush at questions like that.
I didn't know there's a light that departs the human eye
when we leave here. That disappears like a morning.
Like a shadow describing an hour under whatever sun.
There are life forms in the deepest oceans, creatures
with six- and seven-syllable scientific names, existing
without anything like that light entering or leaving

anything like an eye. They remind me of everything
I can't imagine that may be the case. Everything
I don't know that may be a sign of something else.
Roses I sent you tumbled from their vase on the day
of the funeral, an arrangement called Blush Perfection—
wasn't that a sign of something? I like to think so,
though gathering up ruined red roses mostly asserts
that things fall apart, regardless. What happens after
we die? Some rest with a poem in a shirt pocket.

Taos, Lightning

That afternoon we moved through Taos Pueblo,
the oldest continuously inhabited human dwelling
in North America, learning what it is to live together,
a good thing to try and make sense of on a honeymoon.
We crossed light-burnished Red Willow Creek. Skies
had blackened to the south in the direction of Santa Fe.
We ventured into dim shops to handle silver artifacts,
eat frybread, and came out to the first huge droplets

of a thunderstorm. Arrows of lightning rained down
from the clouds above arroyos, star-bright branchings
of no discernible intelligent design loosed and blazing
and vanished in an instant. The strikes were in the hills
above the Taos street where Kit Carson had lived once.
We ducked for cover inside a rental car. You shivered
as I started the engine and rolled down a window. Lit
a cigar I'd bought in Santa Fe, the leaf-scent a thing

a passing Tiwa man said was pleasant and welcome.
All this was years ago, and my memory plays tricks.
Maybe the Tiwa man said nothing but only looked
in our direction—these beings who move as one—
and I learned what humans have always known or
might learn on any given afternoon in New Mexico:
that we are all just trying to come in out of the rain,
visiting for such a brief time under the turning sky.

Homeless Man Reports a Dead Body
by Carrying a Skull into a Florida Publix

—Colin Wolf, *Orlando Weekly*

Imagine him in the act of crossing busy US 1,
a silver shopping cart to slow the murmuration.
See the heat shimmers above the road surface.
See a Maserati swerve. Hear a Bentley brake
hard enough to make the muscles of the heart
speed up. In no time, he is parking the object
on a trash can by a double-door to a Publix.
By the pink-flamingo-themed lottery posters.
Why did he take it? Maybe the eyes called up
long rows of tombstones. His own dear dead
or their histories. One witness says he used it,
the skull, like a hand puppet. One said it stank.
A woman recently emptied of a miscarried son.
She called. And so now a cruiser spills a cargo
of sheriffs in their Ray Ban Aviator sunglasses.
Later that day, another part of the neighborhood,
a van is stuck in drifts and mangroves bordering
a strip club. Under night-marching moon and stars,
the doorjamb of the van hemorrhages arterial-red,
the factory-painted truth that our rough home
is limbed with death in the best of weather.

After the Gauguins

Each was married to someone else and saw things as not
being paradise or perdition but about what you might expect.

She liked sitting quietly for an hour and asked him to travel
to the National Gallery. She wanted him to see that women

in the paintings of Paul Gauguin all have downcast eyes
but no shame. Like butterflies, they have flitted about

before alighting by fires—their black manes driving
the play of flame, at least one scrawny yellow dog

to guard smoke making the glyph for an afterlife.
Who needs the cargo of deliberate ships from Paris

if you're catching sight of Enchantment, deciphering
the codes of existence in blossoming breadfruit trees?

Afterwards, waiting for the metro, he looked down.
Beside the rail, a fat rat the ash-grey color of the skies

where she would be moving for work soon, without him.
After the National Gallery, the Gauguins, he could look

at a rat and glimpse most of what the foreseeable future
comes whizzing through without message or meaning.

The December Night W.A. Mozart Died

His elbows pressed against the bedding, Mozart
raises himself, the tonnage of any life exhausting.
He may be surprised by his own ill health and luck
as he traces piscatorial shadows in a dream of lakes,
hears obbligato and ad libitum in the squalls outside.

Even the maid knows that Herr Mozart is penniless.
The owner of a tavern where he drinks on Thursdays,
Josef Deiner, landlord/bartender at the Silver Snake,
tithed an armful of wood so "dear Maestro" may die
staring into fire-sputterings echoing advent candles.

His wife is there in the ladder-back chair by the bed.
He hallucinates her thumbing nutflesh, the dark arcs
of shattered stuff become a carpet of musical notes.
Finally, he sees a resemblance to the Holy Mother
then a woman at court he passed out beside once.

Soon there will be no more fits of coughing, no more
operas. No more tankards of ale on endless credit on
Thursdays and no more dismissible royal gatherings.
Fire being fire, some part finds fuel where there is
none and displays on the wide-board wood floor.

for Dave Eggar

A Fisherman Casts His Net at Sunset

Maybe he's not in the right place, not a fisher of men,
but he raises a bible of black net in praise of mariners
and passerine birds and the luck of the long last breath.

The sky is streaked blood-of-the-poet red and an indigo
like the umbra at the center of some fireworks displays.
The waters of the inlet translate all of this as darkness.

Again, he's landed a memory—sitting on the tail of a
sailfish, working free the barb in the mouth of the fish
as his father or an uncle shout instructions in Spanish.

Again, he feels the doomed fish rise as big as a Prius.
Recalls belligerent weight and the blind faith of gills.
Brave respirations on a bloody boat floor after hope

of deliverance had gone. Now an iPad with ear buds
plays classic rock. He turns it up. Hears himself sing
aloud the Jackson Browne song about taking it easy.

Motel America

The first thing I heard that afternoon after sex
was that Bonnie Parker of Bonnie & Clyde fame
had *Roy* and *Bonnie* tattooed in two blue hearts on

the inside of her right thigh. Shocking for a woman
in the 1930s and a detail you might not expect, given
she was with Clyde Barrow for most of her adult life.

Sharing trivia like this while lying naked on a bed
was her declaring she was bad too: bad to be here
and married. She was saying that, since my name

was Roy, I shared something with Bonnie Parker.
Small wonder that the light in the room loved her
and the way she spoke not so much about herself

but about the bread and the knife of us, the need.
And I learned again there are all kinds of intimacy.
And that some may unfold at the Motel America,

"ranked #17 of 37 hotels in Ensenada, Mexico
on the Trip Advisor"—she wasn't beautiful or
young the afternoon she rattled off that love

is having 9 horses and 8 stalls. Meaning
that the heart is always arrow-pierced and
blue. Bigger than any one tattooed name.

Rock Springs

Jim Fulford drove an old logging road the wrong way
into a mining operation, the hysteria of heavy equipment
and badlands-Wyoming addled by an abundance of lighting,
a night-as-day industrial scene, which he knew was a mistake,
our being shunted off to road's edge by the monster haulers.

And so he pulled off, saying Someone else drive a while.
Which is how I wound up behind the wheel of a Chevy van
five miles outside Rock Springs, Wyoming on the 4th of July—
hearing a voice rise above the mining racket, one passenger
shaken awake to ask, Where in the pluperfect hell are we?

Everywhere, earth-movers trafficked unmarked road.
They shook the van, the other riders, a dog named Yeti
who had good-naturedly slobbered on me for days now.
I got in behind the wheel, though all I knew to do was
turn around and try and dodge the great black wheels.

I did an about-face in the root-and-core mist of the place
and drove until I found a convenience-store parking lot
by an onramp for I-80. I pulled in. Killed the engine.
There are times someone has to decide what's next.
I decided we would drink beer and watch fireworks

Wyoming locals loosed above the wreck of the world
they called America. Then the windshield fogged over.
And the windows in the doors. And you couldn't see.
The signage of the convenience-store/filling station
blurred, those vague shapes all the fireworks we got—

Jimmy Fulford and David Pryor and me. And Yeti,
a Great Pyrenees pup nudged us he had to be walked
and so left his pile of dog shit in some pocket of dark
in midnighted Rock Springs, Wyoming: something
we put in the rear-view mirror as we drove away.

The Sexiness of Older People

Why not every joy-toy and thingamajig imaginable,
meaning what's pleasing or acceptable to the rookie

is perfected by hands examining a plural happiness.
Antediluvian Clark Gable can bed Marilyn Monroe,

even with leg tremors and having to start stop start,
cracking his major-movie-star smile at who we are

and what we thought on the way to boundlessness.
Maybe it's the allusion to movies, but I'm thinking

about the quantum mechanics of starlight-as-DNA,
a chemistry of doggedness, but that isn't it exactly.

I'm thinking of my aunt touching my dead uncle.
He was her husband. I was about to say *her friend*.

A drape of bunting bellying around the catafalque
below a casket a Holiness preacher had pounded—

I remember she leaned over in an act of defense
as if what this is about is protecting one another.

How else to say *Goodbye* after years of sweet sex
and the pleasures of falling asleep together after.

7 Minutes

One afternoon in July in the high desert,
in a fenced part of some acreage, stallions
fought to the death. Artesian, the younger,
literally sashayed; and Snowcap, the rival,
much older, wasn't yet blind but it was close.
They struggled for the mare. And for a place
at the watering hole. I don't want to reduce

nineteen seventy-seven to seven minutes—
I ran into David Pryor at a poetry reading
in Columbus, Ohio and he brought it up.
He recalled it a scorcher of an afternoon
for Bend, Oregon (and Rooster Ranch).
He remembered the electric fence failing.
Something about how paralyzed we were,

witnessing horses slam into the wooden
portion of the fence—which cracked and
speared one of the horses. That had stayed
with him, with David, and for over 40 years.
He asked if I remembered us circling around
to stop them, the stallions; if I recalled seeing
Snowcap start a dance of victory that ended

with him falling dead. David told me
that's the story: how, without warning,
death is here. How the suffering world
turns factual at last, a whirlwinding earth
unmagically settling on the recently fallen.
Something like that. Not his words exactly,
but he was there, and so he could tell you.

FOUR

The Fighting Lady

My parents wanted to bring a sister home from the hospital.
I had been the only child for 7 years. And my father elected
to bribe me with an Every-Boy-Wants-a-Remco-Toy, which

recognized "D Size Batteries (Not Included)". Fired ash-can
depth charges. Had a catapult. A landing boat with a winch.
Box art showed things flying off the warship in all directions—

it's never done, is it: buying a place for ourselves in the world.
And struggling to shake off a feeling there is only so much love.
My ship had a flight deck. Rubber-band-jettisoned Sabre Jets.

Pairs of 5-pointed stars adorned a venting structure midships.
Decals, either side, read *USN* and *856*. There were levers—
but when they brought my new sister, Suzanne, home

from Good Samaritan Hospital, laid her in her bassinet with
the lace fringe that reminded me of the armor of my gift-ship,
I began abandoning my play to sneak a look at the new baby.

Soon, the toy ship was missing parts. The turret still swiveled,
but the big gun had abandoned belching Johnson's Baby Powder,
which I once made waft up to the bassinette as I listened for her,

for noises of satisfaction and joy that were becoming a voice.
Just like that—I'd snapped my fingers, but you can't see me—
the scene is over, our parents are in the earth in a cemetery

in Ohio where autumn still arrives like a thing shot from
a turret as it rotates left then right, left again, to soft crying.

Reckless and Weed-wild

If you were the kind of man that others feared
like Ed Potter (who had been in the penitentiary)
or brother Earl (who read Zane Grey westerns),

you were likely to get shot. Stabbed. No one
in eastern Kentucky would risk a fair fight,
my grandmother said. No one wanted left

unconscious on the soiled floor of the bar.
It seems too simple to be knifed then shot
and die staring at a window of feed sacks.

I was 5 the first time I heard those stories.
And when she finished speaking in tones that
opened the two graves again—ever-deepening

tones ending in her calling out *O lord, O lord!*—
the front of her housedress dark with weeping.
If she got herself under control, I would hear

of forms she filled out. A hospital exam room
as windowless as she imagined a room in Hell.
If I'd been a man, she said more than once.

Home Movies

This life, my uncle said, is a home movie.
There's a sting to talking like that and a pride.
So we hoisted a bedsheet screen. Set up chairs.
And then watched ourselves lobbing snowballs.
Some of the footage filled with globes of breath
breaking apart and then, seconds later, reforming.
A compass needle of faces swiveled toward voices.
Whose idea was it to dress as if December required
grins to complement hearts believing in Santa Claus?
He bought a Kodak Electric 8 Zoom movie camera.
Started hauling it out on holidays. At graduations.
It gave him pleasure to set up the lights and shoot.
Look there. See us take off across a yard laughing
at a deluge of recognition upon hearing your name.
Soon, he made a profession of faith. Was baptized.
For a while he might watch who he was and smile,
but later it pained him to see one Camel cigarette
or a Pabst Blue Ribbon beer can in his hand and so
those impromptu screenings became less frequent—
he may have figured it better to leave no record,
especially on film without exonerating sound.

Angel Wrangling

It's tough, I suppose, to lasso anything living.
Especially a creature hunkered down in an hour
of buttery light carrying Eden like some found coin.

This bright-feathered portent is talk-singing a rendition
of Gregg Allman's "Melissa"—and so quite distracted
with some ghost-Melissa—as if you can categorically

cowboy the Metaphysical, drop your best blue noose
over a shoulders-and-wings upper part of the body
while last sun brazes the grass and groundcover.

Once, this one roadied for the Allman Brothers.
He gives me a look that says *Really, bub? really?*
in effect, weighing in on millennia of human failing.

He deports himself well, this unrepresentative god,
with rope-squeezed chest and flame-flickers for eyes.
I can feel the white lie of a hereafter set like a hook.

1964

All around the painted-concrete walls of Bentley Electronics,
on shelves my father built because no one else could do the job
to his specs, TVs show color or black-and-white programming.
A vertical-hold tube in back of the mahogany-cabinetted RCA
is shot, he says, causing the picture to roll. Other sets are on—
thankfully, all the indicator knobs are set to Channel 7 WHIO.
My old man is actuary of the electronics world. He's tasked
with staving off the entropy in Admiral and Curtis Mathes,
GE and Goldstar, Motorola and Philco, Sanyo and Zenith.
He's never heard of The Beatles but doesn't seem to mind
that I've turned up the volume for *The Ed Sullivan Show*—
the Fab Four are starting to play. My father's spent a week
and a day troubleshooting this badly behaving 25-inch Zenith.
So the question is him taking a break, my father who listens to
Johnny Cash, Patsy Cline, the Grand Ole Opry, to make himself
That Other Father Who Pays Some Attention to What His Kid Likes.
Can he do it? Lennon shakes his hair. Sings he wants to hold some

girl's hand. I haven't a clue what it's about, wanting to hold hands.
I'm ten. I haven't felt vertical-hold misfirings referred to as Love.
My pops has pulled up a stool and seated himself in front of *Ed
Sullivan*. Ed says he finds The Beatles to be polite young men.
My short-haired father gives me The Ol' Chuck on the Shoulder,
drawling *Jaysus!* at the start of the commercial for shave cream.
If grief has a heritage and battle flag and its citizens knock back
shots with Jesus above the dead-eyed lost ones, then this isn't that.
This is the complication of being born here with a story of ships
and travel in the DNA, in the skin before the heart and lungs
begin to slough off the temporal in favor of holding hands
with God or Nothing. This is the day before grief starts.
This is our introduction to John Paul George and Ringo,
mine and my father's, in a shop by a workbench and tools
with which men write a story of cash passing hand to hand.
If getting to live at all is like a great song, somewhere in Ohio
TVs blare a rendition through a 3-inch speaker, and applause.

Red Bridle

High desert. A pond bisected by wire fencing
that should be but isn't electrified. Horses
swimming to the wire from both sides
and a rancher irrigating a field of alfalfa.
Something's wrong. An appaloosa stallion
has crossed the wire. It begins with the rancher
stepping from the ditch. His teardrop-shaped face
fills with the dread of old energies and instincts.
I'm beside a backhoe. Standing with the others.
Something to do, I grab a red bridle. Take off.

In our part of Ohio in the 1950s and 60s,
what death we saw was the television kind.
Kids played together in abandoned orchards
and the world was all right. Appeared to be.
Summers, we spent whole days in the trees.
Between the orchard and a hill by our house,
I found headstones. An abandoned graveyard.
And, you bet, we played between the markers.
Like the poem says: *And death shall have no
dominion.* Not to us, laughing in summer.

The stallions meet like lovers who like it
rough. Then they tear at each other. It's hard
to look away from the part of the animal self
where we fall together as one body. Fence
splinters. An end enters a horse's chest—
I want not to recall the blacks of its eyes.
That the rancher couldn't cry. Then could.
I still see myself holding the red bridle as he
scoops out a shallow grave with a backhoe.
Hard for a one-armed man, but he does it.

Jerusalem Road

In Ohio, roadsides swill cruel winds. Placards
declare *Jesus Saves* and *Abortion Is Murder*

by red white blue tube-neon for the strip club
where (I hear) local women scoop up regulars

with slender-fingered hands with press-on nails.
A street sign out front barks **Jerusalem Road.**

One entertainer is day-shift nurse at the hospital,
another drives for UPS. Night braids half-truths

to the hoods and fenders, F-150s and Silverados,
mirrors of the metal renaming pink cement block.

Those who meet the cover charge tell their story
of making too much eye contact with a stranger

who then whisper-talked them out of fifty bucks
in singles in a room with beer signs on the walls.

Inside, maybe a laid-off worker from Pittsburgh
badmouths Ben Roethlisberger and the Steelers.

Inside, maybe someone calling herself America
has a bad cocaine habit and a case of the blues

so great even the ghost of Joy has left her face.
America strips to rap through ruined speakers.

Once

I had stepped back from your lesson of the heavens.
We'd gone inside. Gotten you into Care Bear pajamas.
You were ready for a story about a pink-blanketed pony.
I began: *She let herself be lifted up and handed the reins.*

And when we finished, you were wide awake. So I put you
on your springed horse Wonder. Always, that giddy-child joy.
The other story that summer was the chemical plant explosion.
Columbus reporters and the Sky-Cam chopper elbowed forward

for a look at flags of smoke and the burned-beyond-all-recognition.
The accident was near where I'd tried to teach you the constellations.
That night, you said, you felt the hard plastic of the Jenny Lind potty
shake. You said you recalled night braiding flames that, later, forced

a frightened neighborhood into lines of cars. *'Splosion!* you offered.
Once, your grandfather Bentley was reading in the john, pants down
in Thule, Greenland under arctic generator light, an aurora borealis,
when a B-52 Stratofortress and H-bomb cargo let down out of fuel.

It shook the Quonset hut john, the impact, but he rode out the jolt.
Think of this when you get where you are going. Celebrate what is
far off and moving as filtered, eclipsed light. Maybe not even light,
by definition, by the time it shakes the dark at your back. I did not

leave you in that Ohio. And now, years later, you tell me an aunt,
90 and counting, has said that she is afraid for your immortal soul.
I've lived far too long hearing explosions like that under a heaven
of stars hotter than hells she imagines from the comfort of home.

The Schwinn American

Go now
I think you are ready.
—William Carlos Williams, "Tract"

My dad who thinks life is nineteen sixty-two
forever and unfolding on Comanche Drive
is uncrating a 20-inch Schwinn American.
Opalescent red and with a coaster brake
and 1.75 middleweight tires. The box reads,
in black italic lettering, ***An all-American!***

A single-bulb brilliance divides, the glow
like a flashlight through a colander. Enough
available light by which to read and discover
that the A31 is offered only as a boy's bike.
He's wrenching away, affixing training wheels,
the $^3/_8$-inch boxed end moving with certainty

and pride as if no one has done this before
in a two-bedroom brick house with a carport
where a father is hovering like the Almighty
above antediluvian Ohio. He's sliced a finger
on the chain guard. Waves a bleeding left hand
in the direction of the ceiling. Swears loudly.

It's Christmas Eve and I'm padding about
in migrating-geese-and-ducks feety pajamas,
out of sight, trying not to let him know I know
that he's just cried out instructions to God
as to what to do with my blankety-blank
red Schwinn blankety-blank American.

A Box of Stars

An unasked-for and inscrutable gift
to get just before Christmas, considering.
Opening it, I see cardbacks are inaccurate.
Not a single constellation's hole-punchings
match the right ascension and declination.
Not even Orion lines up with Betelgeuse.

Ursa Major is "an astronomical bestiary"
and I look up the definition of *bestiary*,
read aloud so that we agree to disagree
about the Universe being a petting zoo.
The problem with gifts and their stories
isn't the unpardonable Pitiable Choice

but that we forget the magnitude of effort
it takes to make anyone feel truly special.
Despite the odds against it, when it works
it's magic on the order of a Virgin Birth.
And it isn't my fault that I hinted strongly
I was ready to learn what spins overhead.

If I count the Myth of Perseus as horseshit,
it's that the winged horse I know sells gasoline.
I read: *Cassiopeia is seven stars of suffering*
because she sometimes hangs upside down.
Now I'm told I don't have to like this gift
only *act* like it until the kids are in bed.

Hard to believe we married, a poor fit
who match up by way of a kind of love
that forgives everything every few days,
a variety of affection in which a house
may fall quiet, the kids asleep at last,
and something spark into place.

Why I Wore Paladin Six-guns to Bed
after the Assassination of John Kennedy

I slept in them, the six-guns. I was learning there are
some things that you love you never stop reaching for.
With the leg tiedowns, it got dicey. Uncomfortable.

My parents had just divorced. And my father was gone.
Some nights, I dreamed I'd been shot. It was the barrel
or grip of a replica Colt Single Action Army .45 revolver

stabbing me in my boy-belly. I'd wake with the Knight
chess piece catching the nightlight glow. Paladin quoted
poetry, but he played chess with a double-barrel derringer

behind his belt buckle. And I recall asking why my hero
stalked men. I knew Lee Harvey Oswald had stalked JFK—
two movies of forfeiture merged at night in my dreams.

The one of the president's assassination, the other
of my unfortunate mother in her bed. In both movies,
I had seen Oswald paraded through a police station:

one of Oswald's eyes was black, his face swollen.
Of course someone stuck a pistol in Oswald's belly
and fired. I remember watching the killing on tv—

later, I was supposed to be in bed, but I walked
the hall of our house like Paladin/Richard Boone
ferreting out villainy. I held the holsters as I passed

Mother's room: so leather noises wouldn't wake her.
I heard gentlemanly Richard Boone breathe a blessing.

Below the Roosevelt Bridge

My cousin Jim makes his way to the white S bridge
spanning the St. Lucie. By the dock in Stuart he points
to the boat traffic moving under a glide of shorebirds.

We're walking a street named for the Seminole chief
betrayed because all's fair in the stealing of a country.
Jim wipes a lens with a Chick-fil-A napkin. Finished,

he frames the penumbra of a dorsal fin, black eyes—
dead eyes. The fish wash up here because it's Florida
and dead fish wash up all the time on Florida beaches.

I don't think, Here's a metaphor for what we overlook.
I do figure that he's opened the Book of Jim to a page
where the indecipherable appears as finned and scaly.

We stop. And hang off each other for a photograph:
a fat stranger frames us with a blue-sky background,
asks if we're brothers. We're looking for my truck—

I tell Jim I parked in shade since it's black, the truck.
I don't want to say I can't remember exactly where.

The Heaven of Dragonflies and Damselflies

By the tap of his walking stick and the wheel noises
of the portable oxygen machine, an audible *tap-whack*
tap-whack, I hear that Chance Locke is going outside.
My pal Chance can't walk his white toy poodle Toto,

though he can witness this Anisoptera's monkeyshines.
The air-show theatrics distract him from matters of fact.
Like that he will be dead soon. Under the bougainvillea,
he said once that the eyes of the Yellow-winged Darter

touch, as with all dragonflies. Chance isn't just another
Floridian who doesn't know damselfly from dragonfly.
Now he waves in my general direction across the grass.
It goes dark, the August rain like a round of applause.

Then, as if someone closed the spigot, the rain stops.
Bluets are back from wherever they go in tempests:
weathering under a frond where a body in motion,
that oldest of winged timepieces, marks the hour.

FaceTime

We have no ritual except I be amazed once more.
First, at the air of accountability that enters rooms

like shadows spreading under trees at the moment
we walk beneath them. In her iPhone's screen light

her face is the perennial glow of late-fallen leaves
pixelating, swimming across distances and the dark.

I'm content. And pleased to see this warrior-woman
who is, quite literally, the consequence of letting go.

Still, there is the reprimand in her memory of noises:
I'm hearing that she remembers me leaving a house

where the pending delight of my sleeping children
should have been more than sufficient to keep me.

Given that last long silence, and what I take to be
a look of forgiveness, I was right to try and atone.

Moving for Work

It was 2005 or 6, summer & I'd moved
from Wisconsin to Florida with my wife.
We bought a house in a gated community

near the ocean. I couldn't have cared less
for beaches. Or for Florida, for that matter.
But one afternoon after rain, the white-zap

of lightning, thunder loud as truck traffic,
three sandhill cranes lifted into rinsed air—
I'm from Ohio, so magic isn't the first or

even the second thing I expect from a day.
A man looked up & pointed to the flyway
for a small poodle by a blood-brown pool.

————————

My wife's cousin N.'s husband J.P.'s pop is a Wise Guy.
J.P. shows us his Tampa house, bought with race-track dough:
framed pictures of the Sands & the Rat Pack, real gold records.
Talk of dealing blackjack in casinos, Ol' Blue Eyes at the Riviera.

We hear that a Disney World artist sculpted J.P.'s pool's mountain,
its grotto & emerald crocs with rows of teeth the size of pasta forks.
Big-screen TV in the living room wall, pictures of a tax-lawyer son,
tops in his class at FSU. J.P. talks e-trades & commodity prices

by the pool, waiting for N. to signal the veal marsala finished.
I warm to J.P.—he tells me about a shooting in a bar he owned,
laying on the details of the blood fountaining, his face owning
a look on my face when he says, *Oh, the guy?—he survived.*

N. waves. J.P. goes in. My wife's from Little Italy, Cleveland.
In '68, she was bridesmaid in their wedding. We're one-day guests,
but J.P. shows us through the sliding-glass doors like we're *paisans*.
He's a great host. So is N. And the veal is, as they say, to die for.

I tear myself away from Kevin Costner's *Wyatt Earp*
to step outside & watch a white contrail plume rise
& Discovery's external fuel tank flash orange

in the sky above Young & Prill Funeral Home
in Stuart, Florida. My neighbor comes out to ask
what I think of Florida, having seen a shuttle launch.

I say, *You bet* & nod because he doesn't need me
to launch into how I wish my country, his country,
would discover the truth about its love of rockets.

He smiles. I smile. Then I point & say, *Right*
over the goddamn funeral home like that says it
& like I know to give death its due. And inside,

a bigger-than-life Wyatt Earp is shooting it out
with a man who wears a look says he knows
he deserves both steady barrels leveled at him,

at his sudden & unrequited interest in mercy.

The Bright and Hungry Future of Hawks

. . . and the explosions
of feathers where blue jays
have been ripped into the bright
and hungry future of hawks . . .
—Bob Hicok, "My Most Recent Position Paper"

Collapsing flakes of dark dust the bite marks
on the remnant lower leaves of a species of oak,

russet leaf edges curving inward like old papyrus.
By the sea walls, breezes furrow the lake surface

and a few deer, thriving in arboretum-like calm,
startle at an impressive wavefall and compass on.

We are not that feast of undergrowth nor are we
the leaf eaters nor the alchemy that sustains them;

nor dawn-veneered pleasure craft in the distance
approaching amphibians hopscotching the reeds.

Nor wind and light trilling a beach where hawks
circle with the discipline of daybreak near water.

Wonder Wheel

A blond woman with a Samsonite suitcase at the border
of a Coney Island ride, a broken-promises look on her face
like she's figured out that she may have to rescue herself.

Look, it's just a photograph I took off the Internet today.
After I decided the United States of America, my country,
is your-fucked-up-brother-in-law stupid. An uber-idiot.

Jim Harrison says the Statue of Liberty needs a necklace
of human skulls—"her great iron lips quivering in a smile"—
and that skulls striking together is the true sound of history.

America, you're like a woman who wants to get reckless
in the Men's Room of a coffee shop. For shits and giggles.
You're pissed off at yourself. And more than a little crazy.

We're on the Wonder Wheel, you bet. And if I like Woody,
it isn't that I excuse anything because his movies are funny,
especially since only one or two early ones made me laugh.

If I consider the teals and goldenrods of the leaves on the
woman's print dress in *Wonder Wheel* to be a bit much,
it's that autumn colors suggest—what else?—falling.

The Death of the Box Turtle

I'm pretty sure that when she was dying
and sang "Amazing Grace" to him, she wasn't
recalling running after him down the long hill
of Comanche Drive, spitting up burst bubbles
of blood from some dark place deep inside her.
He was her grandson. Old Devil, she called him.
The before-and-after photograph of a kid falling

from the top of the playground slide or executing
a dive off a refrigerator-top, educating the knees
of the umpteenth pair of Levi blue jeans
with kneeling in tar and brake fluid blotted
from the carport floor. Once, as a sort of joke,
he tied her apron strings to the slats of her rocker
as she dozed before *Search for Tomorrow*.

When Bobby—that was his name—was 8 or 9,
he would go out and come in, come in and go out,
slamming doors until there was no escaping him.
And he announced his boredom one afternoon
by jimmying a steel crossbar from a swingset
at the edge of the orchard behind our house
and bludgeoning a turtle to death with it—

where the steel had gone in, a shell fracture
revealed bloody interior curves. Bobby and I
recalled the death of the box turtle years later,
after the other wreckage of childhood
had retracted. We were driving back
from my having read poetry for a good fee
at a university in the Midwest. I was buzzing,

full of Merlot and poached salmon. Nothing
could've been further from my mind than
his handiwork come back in the phrase
Granny always liked you best. We were men.

Such things should have been put away long ago,
left to drift like the odor of rotting windfall apples
in orchards at the end of autumn. They hadn't been.

I want to say the turtle died easily, bled out,
the beneficiary of some unexpected grace loosed
like manna from the sky over Kettering, Ohio.
Truth is, its going took forever—someone else
had filled in the turtle's wound with clods of earth,
some plump child perhaps trying to reconstruct something
in his or her image. Maybe some future veterinarian.

I want to say Bobby healed and all that pain fell away,
sloughed like shell a reptile head telescopes in and out of
to touch smell hear see bright Nothing, if nothing else.
But healing is part forgetting, a search for tomorrows.
He didn't heal. He might have, had the song gone on
and Granny Potter, weak of heart, diabetic, come back
from the country of memory, some "holler"—

up from the deathbed of her terribly important one life.
Which, come to think of it, was what she did,
choosing Bobby to sing to before she died:
her piercing *a capella* dirge of "Amazing Grace"
sounding in a hospital room by a creek where turtles
drank (had forever) and trudged off, small,
liminal, pitifully slow in the light.

Palimpsest

Here come x-ray-like images of winged seraphims
flitting about in concrete-block houses of last resort.
Fallout shelters. This is *that* October and *that* 1962.
I'm up past my bedtime. I hand off a piece of paper,
a palimpsest of life in a shelter redrawn with angels
because Ohio may presently be thermonuclear dust.

The presence of angels has to do with the missiles.
Ours. Theirs. All the talk that we're going to war.
1962 is the year I become aware of just being here,
at the highest residential point in Kettering, Ohio—
if you're smart, you don't slide around on spilled beer
in red-brick ranch houses with unforgiving tile floors.

Sometimes I get happy, listening to my father's music,
and, well, just last week I slipped on a little of his beer.
I went down and glimpsed heaven in stars at the edge
of sight. I made a trip to the ER at Good Samaritan
for x-rays. I lack any aptitude for dancing on beer.
Drawings I do these days are valedictions, farewells—

I've read the word *valediction* in a book at school.
And about the alterations in the nuclei of atoms
at Ground Zero. I can say goodbye to Ohio.
But where will I go when I die if it isn't a place
like Kettering? I'm 8½. What I know is that, here,
even stumbling and concussing yourself is dreamlike.

I'm that precocious Bentley kid signs his sketches
before handing them to a mom who files them away
for safekeeping—habit lately with Doom like a slick
floor and grown ups trying to dance on it but falling,
the screams and voices changing being 8½ forever.
And no one caring if you're happy or if you turn 9.

Roy's Prostate Discusses This Dark Hour

You knew, sooner or later, a prostate would speak up.
In the past, Joe's Liver pontificated in *Reader's Digest*.
The right lung started in about his two-pack-a-day habit,
the calamitous inattentiveness of the nineteen-seventies.
I'm as flabbergasted as you that the swamp-like gland
tasked with supplying the seminal fluid wants to talk.

We used to drive to his parents' house, Roy and me.
He'd have the T-top open. Windows cranked down.
I'd feel the Goodyears grab as we'd come to a stop.
We would sit like that in his white Firebird, idling
just under the last stoplight sheathed in Ohio gray,
dashboard electronic-racket signaling our intention

to execute a right-on-red onto his parents' cul-de-sac.
On the 8-track, Gregg Allman would be disappearing
the manic jack-hammering by the state route: *Well, I've*
been out walking. I don't do that much talking these days.
These days, the topsy-turvy nature of reality is the rule
and you don't have to be a genius to see a connection

between the 15-stick biopsy and Donald John Trump:
one is a series of fifteen incisions into suspicious tissue,
the other is the President of the United States of America.
Ohio would be the republic of ghost towns without change,
the usual avalanches of Nothing transfiguring everything.
Rivers manifest mutability, replacing smooth roadways

and bridges with Wreckage, the world in its many parts.
Never mind I whisper *river river river* in my darkness.
Never mind the prostate is a child-fist of blood rivers
or that fictive public speaking requires an audience.
I felt my driver turn up the music in his America,
waiting for the light to change and message Go.

www.ingramcontent.com/pod-product-compliance
Lightning Source LLC
Chambersburg PA
CBHW020256090426
42735CB00009B/1104